Original title:
Horizon Within



Author: Swan Charm

ISBN HARDBACK: 978-9908-1-2611-1
ISBN PAPERBACK: 978-9908-1-2612-8
ISBN EBOOK: 978-9908-1-2613-5

## Tides of the Soul's Journey

Waves crash upon the sandy shore,
Carrying whispers of yore.
Each ebb a lesson, each flow a tale,
Guiding the spirit, through storm and gale.

Stars shimmer in the ocean's embrace,
Reflecting dreams, lost in space.
With every rise, we learn to let go,
Tides we ride, in ebb and flow.

Shells tell stories of the past,
Memories sealed, forever to last.
Within each curve, a life once lived,
In the depths, the heart is healed.

Sunrise paints the dawn anew,
Horizon beckons with skies so blue.
In the stillness, the soul finds peace,
From the chaos, shadows cease.

The journey winds like a river bends,
Every curve, a chance to mend.
A dance of waves, a song of light,
The tides of the soul, a guiding sight.

## Gateways to the Untold

Beneath the arch of twilight skies,
The hidden paths begin to rise.
With every step, a story unfolds,
Through the doorways to the untold.

Whispers linger in the air,
Secrets woven with utmost care.
Each gateway opens, revealing the way,
Towards dreams that never fray.

Shadows dance in the moon's soft glow,
Inviting hearts to come and know.
On the threshold of the night,
Possibilities take flight.

Every corner, a glimpse of grace,
Moments captured in this space.
Through the portals, the heart takes flight,
Unraveling truths within the night.

In the silence, the answers dwell,
Gently weaving a magic spell.
The untold stories, waiting to be,
Unlocking the essence of what we see.

## Whispers of Celestial Paths

Stars convene on a velvet sea,
Illumined whispers set spirits free.
Through the cosmic dance, we wander on,
Celestial paths where dreams are drawn.

Each constellation, a guiding light,
Leading us home through the starry night.
In the quiet, the universe sings,
A symphony of unfathomable things.

Galaxies swirl in an endless trance,
Moonlit shadows weave a mystic dance.
With every breath, the cosmos calls,
In the silence, the heart enthralls.

Stardust dreams upon our skin,
Echoes of where we've always been.
In the embrace of the night’s cool breath,
We find the beauty in life and death.

Whispers linger in the astral vast,
Memories of futures and echoes of past.
Celestial paths entwine our fate,
Guiding souls to the infinite state.

## The Light Beyond the Veil

In the hush of dawn's first light,
Shadows retreat, retreat from sight.
Veils of mystery start to unfurl,
Revealing truths in a waking world.

With every breath, hope ignites,
Illuminating the darkest nights.
Beyond the veil where spirits soar,
A radiant pulse forevermore.

Golden rays through branches weave,
All that we dream, all that we cleave.
In the garden where spirits play,
The light reveals the hidden way.

Hearts awaken to the beauty found,
In the silence, a sacred sound.
Each moment whispers of what is real,
In the light beyond, our souls can heal.

Through the mist, we ever seek,
The glimmering truth in the meek.
With open hearts, we step inside,
To the light beyond, our souls abide.

## Unfolding Mysteries of Tomorrow’s Light

In shadows deep, the secrets hide,
Whispers call where hopes abide.
With every dawn, a story's spun,
Unfolding dreams, a race begun.

Through tangled paths and trails unseen,
We chase the spark, the vibrant keen.
Each heartbeat sings of new delight,
As clocks unwind in soft twilight.

The stars align, their tales anew,
Guiding souls to journeys true.
With every step, we grasp the night,
Unfolding mysteries of tomorrow’s light.

## Beyond the Edge of Dreams

Where shadows dance and echoes play,
The night unveils a hidden way.
Mystic visions twirl and swirl,
Beyond the edge, a dream unfurl.

In realms where silence softly glows,
The heart awakens, gently knows.
With fingertips, we trace the air,
Beyond the edge, our souls laid bare.

The boundary fades, we drift and glide,
On wings of fancy, we confide.
In whispered hopes, our courage beams,
Together we soar beyond our dreams.

## Echoes of Unseen Dawn

Softly breaking, the light will rise,
In whispered tones, the morning sighs.
From shadowed realms, we feel the call,
Echoes of dawn, embracing all.

Each brush of warmth, a gentle kiss,
Whispers of hope, a fleeting bliss.
In tender hues, the world is spun,
Echoes of unseen, forever run.

With every breath, new life takes form,
In quiet strength, we find the warm.
As darkness yields to skies of gold,
Echoes of dawn, our dreams unfold.

## Embrace of the Infinite Sky

Beneath the vast, unending blue,
Our spirits dance, the light breaks through.
In every breath, the freedom sings,
Embrace of sky, the joy it brings.

Across the clouds, our visions soar,
With every gust, we crave for more.
The wind carries our laughter wide,
Embrace of the infinite, our guide.

In twilight's glow, our dreams ignite,
With stars above, we claim the night.
In boundless love, we find our ties,
Embrace of the sky, where spirit flies.

## Secrets Beneath the Twilight

In the hush of the evening glow,
Whispers of dreams begin to flow.
Stars awaken in soft light,
Guardians of secrets, hidden from sight.

Shadows dance on the cool, damp ground,
Echoes of stories waiting to be found.
The moon spills silver on the trees,
A symphony sung by the night breeze.

Crickets sing a soothing tune,
As magic stirs beneath the moon.
Every leaf tells a tale untold,
In the twilight, mysteries unfold.

The world sleeps, yet some still roam,
Searching for the paths to call home.
In the twilight, hearts ignite,
Finding solace in the night.

Secrets linger in every sigh,
Beneath the vast and endless sky.
With each star, a wish takes flight,
In the silence of the twilight's light.

## Reflections of a Far-off Day

In the mirror of time, shadows dance,
Echoes of laughter, a fleeting glance.
Moments captured, forever replayed,
In the heart where memories cascade.

Sunrise painted with colors bright,
Promises woven in morning light.
Each detail sharp, each feeling clear,
A gentle reminder of those held dear.

Clouds drift by, whispers from the past,
Lessons learned that forever last.
In stillness, we ponder our way,
Reflecting on each far-off day.

With every heartbeat, time does flow,
Rippling waters, soft and slow.
Yet in the soul, a flame does stay,
Warming the heart with love's bouquet.

Moments cherished, they gently fade,
Yet forever in us, they are laid.
In every sunrise, a chance to replay,
The reflections of a far-off day.

## Waves of Infinite Potential

At the shore where dreams collide,
Endless horizons stretch wide.
Each wave whispers a secret truth,
A promise held within our youth.

Ripples dance on the ocean's face,
Every splash a new embrace.
In the depths, hope always stirs,
Waves of change, the heart concurs.

Embrace the tide with open arms,
Feel the pull of nature's charms.
As the sea calls, we must engage,
Writing our stories on each page.

Infinite paths lie just ahead,
By the waves, our spirits are led.
In each crash, a chance to grow,
Infinite potential within the flow.

With each ebb and every flow,
Bravery blooms, and courage grows.
Waves embrace our every quest,
Infinite potential, we are blessed.

## The Canvas of Unfurling Futures

In the quiet of dawn’s first light,
A canvas waits, pristine and bright.
With every brushstroke, dreams take flight,
Coloring visions with sheer delight.

Each hue tells tales of hopes and fears,
Echoing laughter along with tears.
Future possibilities boldly sing,
As we create and paint our spring.

The palette shifts with every thought,
In patterns, destiny is sought.
With each stroke, we shape our fates,
In the gallery where time awaits.

Lines intertwine, merging as one,
Crafting a journey just begun.
The canvas stretches far and wide,
Unfurling futures we cannot hide.

Dream boldly, let your spirit soar,
On this canvas, forever explore.
Embrace the journey, bright and pure,
For every future, we can assure.

## A Symphony of Distant Shores

Waves whisper secrets, soft and low,
Melodies carried by the wind's flow.
Stars glimmer bright, across the sea,
Each note a journey, wild and free.

In twilight's glow, horizons blend,
The ocean's tune begins to bend.
Crafted by time, it swells with grace,
In every ripple, love we embrace.

Sailors dream of lands unseen,
Charting courses through the green.
With every tide, a new refrain,
In nature's choir, joy and pain.

A compass spins, both wild and grand,
Adventures waiting on distant sand.
Lighthouses gleam, guiding the heart,
Together we'll roam, never apart.

As night descends, the waves unite,
In the symphony of starry light.
Each shore a promise, silent calls,
Together, we conquer, together, we fall.

**The Threads of Celestial Weaving**

In night's deep fabric, dreams entwine,
Stars stitch together, a pattern divine.
Galaxies dance, with colors so bold,
Crafting the stories that time has told.

Each twinkle a whisper, secrets unfold,
Adventures in starlight, daring and cold.
With every pulse, a thread we weave,
A tapestry rich, in which we believe.

Nebulas bloom in blossoms of light,
Ancient remnants of cosmic flight.
We grasp at wonders beyond our sight,
In the loom of the heavens, pure delight.

As midnight beckons, hearts align,
In celestial patterns, we intertwine.
Guided by starlight, hand in hand,
Upon this vast, enchanted land.

Eons collide, fate takes its stride,
The universe watches with pride.
In every thread, we find our song,
Together in harmony, we belong.

## In Search of the Luminous Path

Footsteps wander through shadows cast,
In search of a light that glimmers at last.
Whispers guide us through the night,
Promising hope, a future bright.

Secrets abound in the moon's soft glow,
A pathway unfurls where dreams freely flow.
With every step, the darkness declines,
Illuminated truths, like stars, brightly shine.

With courage as our steadfast guide,
We travel onward, hearts open wide.
The luminous path, an endless quest,
Leads to a place where we find rest.

In quiet moments, we'll make our stand,
And build a future, hand in hand.
For in each journey, wise souls tread,
The light we seek lies just ahead.

Together we'll shine, dispelling the night,
Finding our way in the moon's silver light.
In search of those dreams, we won't lose sight,
Embracing the magic that feels so right.

## Uncharted Territories of the Soul

Venture beyond what eyes can see,
Into the depths where spirits roam free.
In the labyrinth of thoughts, we explore,
Mapping emotions, craving for more.

Each heartbeat echoes, a rhythmic sound,
In the vast unknown, we stand our ground.
Through shadows and light, we bravely tread,
Claiming the paths where angels have led.

Whispers of wisdom, secrets unfold,
Unearthing treasures, more precious than gold.
In uncharted realms, we seek and find,
The beauty of being, both gentle and kind.

With every heartbeat, we stitch our tale,
Resilient and strong, we will not fail.
In the tapestry woven from love and strife,
We write our stories, weaving through life.

For in these territories, we come alive,
Nurtured by challenges, we thrive.
With open hearts, we will discover,
The uncharted soul, a true lover.

## The Spirit of the Open Sky

Above the rolling hills, they soar,
A dance of clouds, forevermore.
With whispered winds, their freedom calls,
In vast embrace, the spirit sprawls.

The dusk paints gold on feathers bright,
As shadows fall, they greet the night.
In silent flight, they seek the dawn,
With every breath, their essence drawn.

Beneath the stars, they find their way,
Through azure dreams, by night and day.
The open sky, their sacred home,
In endless realms, they freely roam.

## Whims of the Celestial Wanderer

A comet streaks, a moment's grace,
With tales of light, it quickens pace.
The galaxies hum a soothing song,
In cosmic depths, where dreams belong.

A nebula swirls in vibrant hues,
Whispers of secrets in cosmic views.
Each twinkle holds a story untold,
Of love and loss, of visions bold.

Through stellar seas, the wanderer glides,
Chasing shadows where wonder resides.
In the tapestry of night, they weave,
With every heartbeat, we believe.

## The Unfolding of Inner Light

In silence deep, the heart's pulse glows,
A gentle warmth, as the spirit grows.
Within the stillness, a spark ignites,
Illuminating the darkest nights.

With every breath, we start to see,
The hidden paths that set us free.
Unraveling layers, truth takes flight,
As shadows dance in the inner light.

Awakening whispers, a guiding hand,
Leading us to a promised land.
In every moment, the light unfolds,
Revealing treasures, forever bold.

## Echoes of the Ether

In the vast embrace of twilight's glow,
The echoes sing of tales below.
Whispers carried on the breeze,
Secrets shared among the trees.

Through windswept paths, the voices play,
Reminding us of life's ballet.
In every sigh, a story flows,
A symphony of highs and lows.

The ether holds both joy and pain,
In gentle rhythms, the heart's refrain.
A labyrinth of sounds divine,
In each echo, our souls entwine.

## Seeking the Forgotten Skies

In twilight's embrace, we search for grace,
Whispers of stars call from their place.
The echoes of dreams long lost in time,
Guide us to realms where hope can climb.

Beneath the vastness, our spirits soar,
Through shadows and light, forevermore.
We chase the tales the ancients wrote,
On wings of memories, we gently float.

The canvas above, a tapestry bright,
Holds secrets of day and whispers of night.
With every sigh, a wish released,\nWe seek the skies
where hearts find peace.

In silence, the cosmos sings our name,
A dance of souls, forever the same.
Through age-old paths, we wander wide,
In search of horizons where dreams abide.

The stars align to share their glow,
Guiding lost hearts through ebb and flow.
In seeking the skies, we find our kind,
The forgotten whispers that love designed.

## The Pulse of the Infinite

In the heart of time, a rhythm flows,
A cosmic beat, where eternity glows.
Each moment a pulse, each breath a gift,
In the dance of existence, our spirits lift.

Stars stir awake, their light like a sigh,
Echoes of life in the vast, dark sky.
Every heartbeat a promise, a bond so tight,
In the pulse of the infinite, we find our light.

Waves of creation, crashing and swell,
In silence, the universe weaves its spell.
Through galaxies spinning, we chase the pace,
In every heartbeat, we find our place.

Fleeting seconds in a timeless sea,
Hold the memories of you and me.
With every rhythm, our souls entwine,
In this pulse of forever, we brightly shine.

As shadows fade and dawn breaks anew,
The infinite echoes a love so true.
In each breath we take, the cosmos sings,
The pulse of the infinite, where belonging brings.

## Tomorrows Yet to Unravel

Through winding roads of hopes and fears,
Tomorrow beckons with whispers and cheers.
Each step we take, a path yet drawn,
In the light of change, we are reborn.

Promises woven in the threads of fate,
Hold dreams unspoken, it's never too late.
With courage in hearts, we face the unknown,
In the garden of time, our seeds are sown.

Moments collide, and colors blend,
The canvas of life can curve and bend.
With visions of greatness, we paint our way,
Into the dawn of a brighter day.

The shadows linger, yet light breaks through,
In tomorrows yet to unravel, we find what's true.
Each heartbeat a whisper, each star a guide,
In this voyage of time, we shall abide.

From dusk till dawn, the journey unfolds,
With stories of dreams and the brave, the bold.
In the tapestry of life, we find our call,
As tomorrows unravel, we rise, we fall.

**Threads of the Cosmic Weave**

In the loom of the universe, we find the thread,
A tapestry woven where dreams are spread.
Each life is a stitch in the fabric so grand,
Connected by fate, by a delicate hand.

Colors of stories interlace and twine,
The essence of being, profound and divine.
As time flows softly, the patterns emerge,
In the dance of creation, our spirits surge.

Through light and through shadow, we wander and roam,
In the heart of the cosmos, we find our home.
Threads of connection bind hearts and minds,
In the weave of existence, true magic unwinds.

A symphony rising, notes woven with care,
Each voice a reminder, we're never bare.
Together we stand, a chorus of light,
In the threads of the cosmic, we ignite the night.

As the fabric of time continues to sway,
We craft our own story, come what may.
In the weave of the cosmos, we're endlessly spun,
Bound by the threads, united as one.

## Light Footsteps on Time’s Shore

Gentle waves kiss the sand,
Whispers of memories unfold.
Footprints vanish in the tide,
Stories of ages untold.

Seagulls dance in the fading light,
Breathing in the salty air.
Each moment a fleeting sight,
Carried on currents so rare.

With every step, we leave behind,
Echoes of laughter and tears.
The past entwined with the wind,
As we sail through our years.

The sun dips low, a golden sphere,
Painting the sky with its glow.
Time's shore whispers, calm and clear,
Embracing all we do know.

In the twilight, we find our way,
Guided by stars in the night.
Light footsteps will always stay,
Fading but never out of sight.

## Radiance of the Unseen

In shadows deep, light will seep,
Illuminating paths once lost.
Hope flickers where hearts still keep,
Dreams shining, no matter the cost.

Whispers carried on the breeze,
As secrets dance in the air.
Moments of joy bring us ease,
In the silence, love is rare.

Unseen threads weave through our lives,
Binding us in gentle grace.
In the dark, the spirit thrives,
Radiance found in every face.

Each heartbeat is a spark divine,
Revealing truths we often miss.
In the stillness, our souls align,
Bringing forth an inner bliss.

A glow within, a guiding flame,
Igniting courage to depart.
In unity, we'll stake our claim,
To find the light within the heart.

## Stars that Speak of New Tomorrows

In the night, the stars align,
Flickering tales of what is near.
Each twinkle a silent sign,
Of hope that whispers softly here.

Galaxies swirl like dreams unbound,
Cradling wishes made in flight.
From depths of space, wisdom found,
Guides our hearts toward the light.

Constellations tell of journeys,
Paths untraveled, yet to tread.
Mapping out our destinies,
With dreams that dance in our head.

In every shadow, light does dwell,
Encouraging steps yet to take.
Stars beckon, casting their spell,
In their glow, new dawns awake.

The universe, a canvas vast,
Each star a promise, a new day.
In the dark, the future's cast,
Guided by their brilliant sway.

## Celestial Compass of Dreams

Guided by the northern star,
We venture far from the known.
In the night, we carry scars,
Yet our hearts, like seeds, are sown.

The moon's embrace, a soothing balm,
Nurtures hopes that dare to soar.
In silence, we find our calm,
As dreams whisper from the shore.

Galaxies spin, our minds alight,
Infinite paths stretch ahead.
Every choice, a chance to write,
A story of stars, a thread.

In the heavens, our voices rise,
Singing songs of our desires.
A tapestry of endless skies,
Woven with our deepest fires.

So trust the compass of your heart,
For dreams are guides through the dark.
In every end, there's also start,
Celestial journeys leave a mark.

## Embracing the Vast Unknown

In shadows where whispers dwell,
We step forth with hearts aglow.
Each step a tale yet to tell,
In the vast unknown we row.

Stars above, a guiding light,
Their spark ignites our brave flight.
We cast aside the fear of night,
Embracing dreams with pure delight.

The winds speak secrets and sigh,
Carrying hopes on their wings.
We soar beyond the questioning sky,
To find the joy that freedom brings.

Mountains loom, yet we stand tall,
Roots deep in courage and trust.
Through barriers we'll break and crawl,
Rise above, and turn to dust.

As we explore each twist and bend,
Our spirits dance with every beat.
In the unknown, we find a friend,
In every challenge, we meet.

## Paths Mapped by the Soul's Compass

Journeys begin in quiet repose,
In stillness, paths are drawn.
The soul whispers, gently flows,
Guiding where dreams are born.

Footprints fade, yet we move on,
With the compass in our heart.
Through dusk till the break of dawn,
Every end is a fresh start.

Through wild woods and shining streams,
We walk the trails of insight.
Embracing both the hopes and dreams,
We find beauty in the fight.

In the thickets, truth unveils,
With every turn, we rediscover.
The path is shared; the spirit prevails,
As we connect one to another.

Guided by the stars above,
We chase horizons wide and free.
With every step, we taste the love,
Of a life lived fully, joyously.

## The Luminescence of Uncharted Realms

In colors bright, the world awakens,
Where dreams are forged in silent halls.
Uncharted realms, our hearts unshaken,
Draw us to adventure's calls.

Through forests thick and fields of gold,
We wander free, spirits ablaze.
Every tale that is retold,
Illuminates our hidden ways.

The glow of dusk paints soft the skies,
As we uncover hidden truths.
With every secret that we prize,
We age like vintage, youthful youths.

In this luminescence, we arise,
Learning wisdom from the stars.
Together navigating skies,
Transforming shadows into bars.

And as we journey towards the light,
The unknown beckons like a flame.
With courage, we will root our flight,
In realms where nothing is the same.

## Dreams Scattered Like Stardust

At midnight’s veil, dreams drift and sway,
Like starlit whispers on the ground.
In cosmic dance, they weave and play,
In the quiet night, they’re found.

With every heartbeat, secrets trace,
A tapestry of hopes and fears.
Each shimmering glance, a gentle embrace,
Collecting all our silent tears.

Beneath the canopy of night,
Fantasies spiral, take their flight.
Into the unknown, through endless sights,
We gather strength to seize the light.

Like scattered stardust on a breeze,
We unite our dreams, diverse and wide.
In harmony, they swirl with ease,
Our deepest longings as our guide.

When dawn arrives, they softly fade,
But in our hearts, they'll never stray.
From dust to dream, we're never afraid,
To chase tomorrow’s bright array.

**Embracing the Light of New Beginnings**

In the dawn's soft glow, hope ignites,
Whispers of change take gentle flight.
Each step forward, shadow shed,
New paths await where dreams are led.

Colors bloom in morning's grace,
A canvas bright, each new embrace.
Clarity follows as doubts fade,
With every choice, a journey made.

The past may linger, yet we rise,
With open hearts beneath wide skies.
A spark within us, fierce and bright,
Together we shall embrace the light.

Turning pages, we start anew,
In every moment, possibilities accrue.
The world spins ‘round with endless chance,
Awakening dreams through every dance.

So here we stand with arms stretched wide,
Embracing choices, no need to hide.
In the tapestry of life we weave,
With every heartbeat, we shall believe.

## The Unwritten Scrolls of Destiny

In the quiet folds of time's embrace,
Lies the story yet to trace.
Every choice, a thread we weave,
In the silence, we believe.

Pages blank, like winter's snow,
Await the ink for tales to flow.
Fingers poised on fate's design,
In whispered thoughts, our dreams align.

Every moment, a chance to start,
Crafting paths that touch the heart.
With courage bold, let shadows part,
In every beat, we play our part.

The future calls with siren's song,
Tempting hearts to dance along.
With every breath, the ink will spill,
On unwritten scrolls, we feel the thrill.

So pen your truths and chase the light,
For destiny waits, a wondrous sight.
Together we shape what’s yet to be,
In the unwritten scrolls, we find our key.

## Dreams Adrift on Windy Seas

Once upon a twilight breeze,
Dreams set sail on endless seas.
With every wave, they rise and fall,
Echoing soft, a siren's call.

Guided by the stars above,
Wandering hearts pursue their love.
Through storms that lift and clouds that weep,
They chase the visions, bold and deep.

The horizon glows with promise bright,
Painting the sky in hues of light.
Anchors cast in seas of hope,
As shadows wane, we learn to cope.

Each gust of wind a tale unspun,
Of journeys taken, battles won.
With open sails and spirits free,
We navigate the mystery.

So let your heart be the guiding star,
As dreams drift near and far.
On windy seas where love may roam,
We find our way, we find our home.

## A Carried Promise in the Breeze

A promise lingers on the air,
Whispers weaving everywhere.
In every rustle, soft and sweet,
The heartbeat of the world, a beat.

Through branches swaying, secrets share,
Stories murmured without care.
In the breeze, dreams intertwine,
Winds of change, a gift divine.

Each fluttering leaf, a chance to grow,
Every sigh, the seeds we sow.
With grace we dance in harmony,
As the world sings our symphony.

Trust the promise carried forth,
In the sun's embrace, a new birth.
Nature's voice, in whispers low,
Guiding us where love can flow.

So pause and listen, breathe it in,
In every moment, let life begin.
A promise kept in a gentle breeze,
In love’s embrace, our souls find ease.

## Flickers of Endless Opportunities

In the twilight's gentle glow,
Dreams awaken, seeds we sow.
Each moment a chance to find,
Whispers of hope within the mind.

Paths lay open, wide and free,
A dance of fate waits just for me.
With every step, new doors emerge,
A symphony of life, I shall converge.

In the shadows, light does gleam,
Flickers of joy, a vibrant dream.
Embrace the unknown, take the leap,
Through valleys steep, my heart I keep.

Unfolding stories yet untold,
With courage, I will be so bold.
Infinite choices beckon near,
With open arms, I summon cheer.

So let me wander, let me roam,
In endless opportunities, I find home.

## The Road Less Traveled

Along the winding, silent way,
Where few have walked, I wish to stay.
With every sigh and every turn,
Lessons hide, and passions burn.

Rustling leaves beneath my feet,
In solitude, my heart beats sweet.
A journey forged, a path unique,
In quiet moments, wisdom speaks.

Not every choice is clear and bright,
But shadows dance and whisper light.
Embrace the road that calls to me,
With every step, I'm truly free.

Mountains rise, and rivers flow,
In stillness, seeds of courage grow.
I'll choose the path, though it may bend,
For in its heart, my spirit mends.

The road less traveled beckons near,
A treasure chest of joy and fear.

## Glimmers of a Brighter Tomorrow

In the dawn's embrace, hope ignites,
Each ray of sun, a glimpse of rights.
The world awakens, eager eyes,
Glimmers of dreams beneath the skies.

With tender hands, we build anew,
A canvas bright with every hue.
Together we rise, hearts entwined,
In unity, our strength aligned.

Days may darken, shadows loom,
Yet love will spark, dispelling gloom.
Through storms that rage, we'll find our way,
A brighter path awaits the day.

Hold fast to courage, plant the seeds,
Nurtured by kindness, timeless deeds.
From ashes rise, the phoenix soars,
With every heartbeat, the spirit roars.

In glimmers bright, we share our light,
A promise made: we’ll win this fight.

## The Secret of the Open Sky

Beneath the vast and starry dome,
A secret whispers of its home.
The winds that dance through heights so free,
Invite my heart to simply be.

Clouds drift softly, tales unfold,
In every heartbeat, dreams retold.
The horizon beckons, wide and bright,
In the open sky, I find my flight.

With wings of hope, I soar so high,
Through shifting skies, my spirit flies.
The secret lies in trusting fate,
A dance of joy, I shall create.

For every star that lights the night,
Is proof of strength, will, and insight.
The open sky, a boundless gift,
In cosmic winds, my worries lift.

With open arms, I greet the dawn,
In life's embrace, I carry on.

## The Edge of Endless Possibilities

On the brink of dreams untold,
We stand with hearts so bold.
The horizon calls our name,
A whisper of hope, a flickering flame.

With each step, fears subside,
As we embrace the wild tide.
Limitless paths spread before,
All we need is to explore.

Unwritten tales lie in wait,
A canvas shaped by fate.
Stars align, the time is right,
Venturing forth into the night.

Every heartbeat shares a truth,
Of lost moments and forgotten youth.
The edge is but a starting line,
To realms where dreams entwine.

So let us dance on this thin edge,
With courage as our pledge.
Tomorrow's dawn will paint the sky,
And in its glow, we'll learn to fly.

## Beneath the Celestial Veil

Under a blanket of shimmering stars,
Mysteries linger, hidden afar.
Whispers of the universe softly call,
In the stillness, we hear it all.

Eternal secrets in the night,
Glimmers of hope, pure delight.
Planets dance in silent grace,
Painting dreams in time and space.

Constellations weave their tale,
Guiding souls through shadows pale.
In the silence, we find our peace,
Beneath the veil, a sweet release.

The moonlight bathes the world in gold,
Each heartbeat a story unfold.
In the dark, we seek the light,
Holding dreams through endless night.

Beneath this vast expanse we stand,
With open hearts and open hands.
Together we embrace the sky,
In unity, we yearn to fly.

## Navigating the Waters of Hope

On a vessel carved from dreams,
We sail through life's winding streams.
The compass points to the unknown,
Where seeds of hope have gently grown.

Waves may crash, and storms may arise,
Yet courage fuels our hearts to rise.
Through tempest's roar and tranquil air,
Hope is the anchor that we wear.

With every oar, we push ahead,
Through currents uncharted, we're led.
In the depths of uncertainty,
We find our strength, our unity.

Glistening waters reflect our dreams,
Carried on gentle, flowing streams.
Navigating through ebb and flow,
The journey teaches all we know.

So let us sail on this voyage grand,
With hope as our guiding hand.
In every wave, in every tide,
Together, we will always glide.

## A Canvas of Untold Stories

Each brushstroke tells a tale,
Of laughter, love, and hearts that pale.
Colors splash in wild delight,
Creating worlds both dark and bright.

Silent echoes fill the air,
Whispers of dreams that once were rare.
In every shade, a story flows,
A tapestry of life that grows.

Moments captured in stroke and hue,
Painting the old, embracing the new.
From shadows deep to radiant light,
Every canvas holds a fight.

In this gallery of dreams we roam,
Finding fragments of our home.
With each reveal, a heart transforms,
In artistry, our spirit warms.

So let us paint with wild abandon,
Creating stories, ever random.
A canvas rich with lives explored,
Forever cherished, never ignored.

## The Secret of the Deep Blue

Beneath the waves, a whisper flows,
Secrets dwell where sunlight glows.
Creatures dance in coral light,
Guardians of the ocean's might.

Echoes carry through the tide,
Mysteries the sea can't hide.
In the depths, the silence sings,
Of ancient tales and timeless things.

Waves embrace the moonlit sheen,
Unraveling what once has been.
The deep blue holds its tranquil grace,
A wondrous, hidden, sacred place.

Ripples whisper, secrets shared,
Nature's heart, forever bared.
In the depths, our souls can dive,
Unlocking truth, where dreams survive.

## Notes of Celestial Melodies

Stars alight with tunes profound,
In cosmic dances, joy is found.
Symphonies of night unfold,
Whispers of the brave and bold.

The Milky Way sings tales of old,
Each note a dream, a spark of gold.
Harmony in silence rings,
A universe that gently sings.

Planets waltz in rhythmic spin,
In celestial arms, they draw us in.
Galaxies in radiant swirl,
A cosmic canvas, bright and unfurl.

With every breath, the cosmos sways,
A symphony that lights our ways.
Harmony in starry night,
Guiding us into the light.

## Constellations of the Heart

Within our chest, a map is drawn,
Of dreams and hopes, from dusk till dawn.
Stars align in patterns clear,
Whispers echo, drawing near.

Love's bright flame ignites the sky,
In constellations, spirits fly.
Hearts entwined in vibrant hue,
Forming bonds both pure and true.

Every pulse, a guiding star,
Shining brightly, no matter how far.
Through shadows deep, in night's embrace,
We find our way, our sacred place.

The heart's firm beat, a timeless dance,
In cosmic realms, we take a chance.
Together drawn, our spirits soar,
In love's embrace, forevermore.

## Flights of the Imagination

Wings unfurl, the mind takes flight,
Chasing dreams into the night.
Ideas soar on breezes wide,
In realms where visions gladly bide.

Through forests green and mountains high,
Our thoughts escape, they learn to fly.
Adventures wait in open skies,
A canvas where the spirit lies.

Creativity knows no bounds,
In whispered winds, the magic sounds.
With every leap, the heart expands,
In the universe, we make our stands.

Imagination paints its tale,
On waves of thought, we set our sail.
In every flight, our souls ignite,
Together shining, pure delight.

## Reflections on the Edge of Time

In whispers soft, the moments dance,
Fragments lost, a fleeting chance.
Echoes fade in shadows' play,
As dusk consumes the light of day.

Time's river flows, relentless, wide,
Carving paths where dreams reside.
Glimmers of what was once held dear,
Drift like stars, yet seem so near.

Every heartbeat tells a tale,
Of hope and pain, where sorrows sail.
From the edge, we gaze in awe,
At life's vast canvas, pure and raw.

The past a bridge, the future, a sea,
Waves of change, so wild and free.
In twilight's hush, we seek to find,
The secrets held within the mind.

So let us stand, embrace the light,
As time unfolds, an endless flight.
With courage drawn from depths within,
We'll weave our stories, and begin.

**Awakening to Boundless Skies**

Beneath a sky of endless hue,
The sun ignites, the world renews.
A gentle breath, the morning sings,
As hope alights on silver wings.

Clouds like dreams drift far away,
In the dawn's light, we will sway.
The horizon calls, a whisper sweet,
To chase the stars, feel the heartbeat.

With every step, the earth awakes,
Joy unfolds as the metal breaks.
Infinite blue, a canvas vast,
Each moment cherished, forever cast.

In the embrace of warm sunlight,
Fear dissolves in the day’s first light.
With open hearts, we rise and soar,
To greet the universe, evermore.

So lift your gaze, let wonder reign,
In the boundless skies, we are unchained.
Together we fly, spirits untied,
In this awakening, love is our guide.

## The Language of Celestial Rhythms

Stars whisper secrets, ancient and wise,
In the moon's glow, we hear their sighs.
A symphony hums through the night air,
Echoing dreams beyond compare.

Constellations weave tales up high,
Stories of time that never die.
In every pulse, a cosmic beat,
An endless dance, magnetic and sweet.

The planets align, a cosmic waltz,
In silence profound, divine and exalt.
We are but notes in this grand score,
Vibrating hearts, forever to explore.

Galaxies swirl in a brilliant embrace,
In the dark, we find our place.
With every glance, we touch the unknown,
In the depths of the sky, love has grown.

So listen close to the astral tune,
Where life unfolds beneath the moon.
In harmony's glow, we will find a way,
To dance with the stars, night or day.

## A Map of Unwritten Destinies

On parchment soft, our dreams take flight,
Charting paths through the dark of night.
Each line a whisper, a choice to make,
A journey woven, for hope's own sake.

In the silence, futures unfold,
Stories woven in threads of gold.
With every heartbeat, a dream ignites,
Guiding souls to new heights.

Each twist and turn, a lesson learned,
For every heart that ever yearned.
In the tapestry of chance we find,
The pulsing rhythm of the divine.

Ink spills truth on the page so bare,
In every journey, we lay ourselves bare.
From choice to choice, we shape our fate,
In this grand design, we navigate.

So pen your dreams with courage bold,
Each story unique, each heart of gold.
For in this map, we are truly free,
Navigating life's great mystery.

## Reaching for the Cosmic Embrace

In the hush of night's quiet song,
Stars beckon where we belong.
Hands lifted to the velvet sky,
Dreams awaken, we yearn to fly.

Galaxies whisper, secrets unfold,
Stories of warmth amidst the cold.
Each twinkle a heart reaching high,
A cosmic dance, we're born to try.

Infinite wonders, wide and deep,
In the cosmos, our souls don't sleep.
Like comets racing, bright and bold,
We leave footprints in stardust gold.

Time bends softly, a gentle sway,
Guiding us through night and day.
In this vastness, we chase our dreams,
Together, stitched in stellar seams.

Embrace the cosmos, pure delight,
In every heartbeat, we ignite.
The universe calls, we take our place,
In the unending cosmic embrace.

## The Dance of Time and Space

Waltzing through moments, soft and sweet,
Time tiptoes, a rhythmic beat.
Stars and planets spin around,
In this dance, life’s beauty found.

Gravity pulls, a silent tune,
Under the watchful eye of the moon.
Each second glimmers like a spark,
Lighting the pathway through the dark.

Eons weave in a patterned thread,
Connected dreams of the living and dead.
The past a shadow, the future a sigh,
In this dance, we laugh and cry.

With every heartbeat, we glide along,
A rhythm that's ancient, a pulse so strong.
Together we move, through space’s embrace,
Lost in the magic of time and place.

Yet, still we reach for what lies ahead,
With hopes and wishes, dreams that are fed.
In the dance of time, we find our grace,
And weave our stories across the space.

## Promises Carved in Starlight

Fingers trace the night’s canvas wide,
Promises shimmer, a love undenied.
Carved in starlight, hopes align,
Eternal vows in the cosmic design.

Every twinkle holds a secret dear,
Whispers of love we long to hear.
Dreams of forever beneath the skies,
In the universe, our spirits rise.

Galaxies spinning, stories collide,
With every heartbeat, we take the ride.
Moments etched in the vast unknown,
Hand in hand, we’ll never be alone.

In starlit nights, our souls ignite,
Burning bright in the silken twilight.
Promises weave like threads of gold,
In the tapestry of love, we’re bold.

Through cosmic storms, we stand as one,
Chasing horizons, until we’re done.
In the end, like stars, we’ll remain,
Our love a promise, forever unchained.

## Tracing the Arc of Infinity

In echoes of whispers, we journey far,
Tracing infinity, guided by stars.
Time spirals, bends, and twists anew,
In the dance of existence, just me and you.

Every heartbeat, a bridge to the vast,
Moments that linger, memories cast.
Light years apart, yet so close at heart,
In this journey, we play our part.

The universe shifts, but love remains,
Through infinite arcs, we break the chains.
Together we sail on waves of grace,
Finding forever in this sacred space.

Stars echo stories, in glimmers bright,
Mapping our souls like constellations in flight.
Each line drawn in cosmic lore,
Unfolds the path to forevermore.

As we trace the arc, hand in hand,
In the vast expanse, we make our stand.
Eternal seekers of what’s divine,
Infinite hearts forever entwined.

## Tapestry of Celestial Threads

In the night, stars gleam bright,
A woven tale of cosmic light.
Threads of silver, whispers low,
Guiding dreams where wonders flow.

Galaxies twirl in quiet dance,
Each point a spark, a fleeting chance.
Nebulas bloom in colors rare,
A tapestry, beyond compare.

Time flows gently, a river wide,
In this vastness, hope abides.
Hearts entwined in the stellar sea,
Boundless love, eternally free.

Comets race through velvet skies,
Casting wishes, cosmic sighs.
Every thread, a story spun,
As the universe comes undone.

So take a breath, feel the night,
Let your spirit take to flight.
In this tapestry, we are one,
Beneath the gaze of the eternal sun.

**A Journey Beyond the Recognized**

Beyond the edge of seen and known,
A path unfolds, the seeds are sown.
With every step, the heart explores,
Unwritten tales, open doors.

Mountains rise, their peaks embrace,
The whispers of the unknown space.
In shadows deep, light finds a way,
To guide the spirit, come what may.

Rivers flow, in currents wild,
Where every wave, a dream beguiled.
In the silence, answers sing,
In each heartbeat, a new beginning.

The horizon calls, a beckoning light,
A promise waits beyond the night.
With courage, we traverse the veil,
Embracing each and every tale.

So let us wander, hand in hand,
In this adventure, we shall stand.
Beyond the recognized, we rise,
To touch the truth, to claim the skies.

## Whispers From the Edge of Infinity

In the void, where silence breathes,
Echoes weave where time deceives.
Each whisper dances on a breeze,
A glittering realm that seeks to please.

Stars align in secret ways,
Painting stories through timeless days.
Bridges built from hope and light,
Lead us further into the night.

In the stillness, dreams take flight,
Carried forth past mortal sight.
The edge of infinity calls us near,
To listen closely, to feel no fear.

Galaxies fade, yet never die,
In every end, a new reply.
The whispers linger, soft and true,
A promise awaits in shades of blue.

So close your eyes, embrace the sway,
Let the whispers guide your way.
For in the edge of vast unknown,
We find the truths we've always known.

## Where Dreams Touch the Sky

In twilight's glow, dreams take form,
Whispers rise, a heart reborn.
Beneath the stars, we draw the line,
Where wishes bloom, and fate aligns.

Each step we take, a dance of light,
In fields of hope, we spread our flight.
The clouds below, a soft embrace,
A cradle of dreams in a timeless space.

With open hearts, we reach so high,
Beyond the reach of the endless sky.
In every heartbeat, a promise glows,
Where dreams take root, and courage grows.

So let us soar, ignite the night,
With stardust dreams, our spirits bright.
Together we'll chase, forever free,
To where our dreams touch eternity.

As starlit tales begin to weave,
In this moment, we believe.
With every breath, the sky unfolds,
A canvas vast, our dreams retold.

## Beyond the Veil of Time

In whispers soft, the moments blend,
Fleeting echoes, where dreams ascend.
Each heartbeat marks a silent flight,
Through timeless realms, we chase the light.

Beneath the stars, where secrets sigh,
A tapestry woven, the low and high.
Threads of memory, both sharp and clear,
Draw us closer, year after year.

The past entwined with futures bright,
A dance that twirls in endless night.
We lift our gaze, horizons wide,
Beyond the veil, where hopes abide.

In every tear, the lessons rise,
Silent wisdom, the ancient ties.
With every step, a road untold,
We wander forth, both young and old.

As time unwinds, our spirits soar,
In the embrace of evermore.
Together we weave the fabric fine,
In this journey, beyond the line.

## The Light Beyond the Shadows

In darkest nights, a glimmer glows,
A beacon bright, where courage flows.
Within the depths, we seek the spark,
To lift our hearts from doubt's stark arc.

Beneath the weight of whispered fears,
A flicker shines, through all the years.
It breaks the chains and clears the way,
Inviting us to greet the day.

The xylem of dreams, in silence sown,
With roots of hope, our strength has grown.
In every shadow, light finds space,
Revealing truth with gentle grace.

Together we rise, hand in hand,
Reaching for light, making a stand.
In unity, our spirits sing,
In harmony, we feel the spring.

Let go of doubts, embrace the shine,
For in the light, our lives entwine.
There's beauty found in every glance,
In the light beyond, we find our chance.

## Dancing on the Threshold of Light

On the edge of dawn, we take a stance,
With every heartbeat, we start to dance.
The world awakens in hues so bright,
As dreams emerge from the shroud of night.

With gentle steps, we sway and spin,
Unfurling hope from deep within.
Each movement whispers tales of old,
Of love and laughter, both brave and bold.

In the soft embrace of morning's glow,
We cast off chains, let joy bestow.
Through twists and turns, our spirits rise,
In this fleeting moment, we touch the skies.

With the rhythm of life beneath our feet,
We find the strength in each heartbeat.
In unity, our souls unite,
Dancing together, pure delight.

So let the light guide every sway,
For every dawn brings a brand new day.
On the threshold, where shadows fall,
We celebrate the light through it all.

## Embracing the Unknown

In silence, we stand, hearts open wide,
To the mysteries waiting, just outside.
With courage drawn from deep within,
We step into realms where dreams begin.

The road ahead is veiled in mist,
Each path unknown, a chance, a twist.
With every heartbeat, we dare to explore,
The beauty of life that lies in store.

Embrace the chaos, let your spirit soar,
For in the unknown, there's so much more.
Each moment a chance, each breath a gift,
In the flow of time, our souls uplift.

With hands outstretched, we gather light,
In shadows cast, we find our might.
With open hearts, we greet the dawn,
In every challenge, a chance reborn.

So let us walk where the wild winds blow,
Embracing all that we do not know.
In unity, we'll find our way,
With faith in tomorrow, come what may.

## Pathways to the Cosmic Light

Beneath the vast and starry dome,
We wander far, we seek our home.
Each whispered wind, a guiding spark,
Illuminates the haunting dark.

Through meadows bright, where shadows play,
We chase the dawn, we greet the day.
With every step, our spirits soar,
Towards the light, forevermore.

Galaxies dance in rhythms slow,
Secrets lie in the heavens' glow.
With stardust hearts, we journey wide,
In cosmic paths, we dare to glide.

Through twisting trails of ancient lore,
We find the keys to open doors.
Past realms unknown, we weave our fate,
In every heartbeat, we create.

So let us wander, hand in hand,
Across this vast and timeless land.
For in the light, we find our way,
Together, we'll embrace the day.

## A Symphony of Endless Skies

In twilight's hush, the heavens sigh,
As colors blend and spirits fly.
The breeze, a song of sweet delight,
Invites us forth into the night.

Stars twinkle like notes in the air,
A symphony beyond compare.
With every glance, we feel the tune,
As galaxies waltz with the moon.

The clouds, they part, revealing dreams,
Where starlight flows in gentle streams.
We listen closely, hearts in thrall,
To nature's hymn, a timeless call.

With every moment, whispers rise,
In harmony, beneath the skies.
An endless dance of light and grace,
A cosmic waltz, our sacred space.

Embrace the night, let spirits soar,
With every note, we seek for more.
In unity, we sing our truth,
A symphony of ageless youth.

## The Realm of Eternal Wanderings

In distant lands, we roam and glide,
Through valleys deep, with hearts open wide.
Endless paths await our tread,
A tapestry where dreams are spread.

Mountains rise and rivers flow,
In every turn, new wonders grow.
The call of adventure fills the air,
With every breath, we find our flair.

Through forests lush, where echoes play,
We dance with shadows, night and day.
In timeless realms, we chase the sun,
As tales of old and new are spun.

With every star, a story we weave,
In every moment, we believe.
For wandering is our sacred rite,
In the realm of eternal light.

So let us journey, hand in hand,
Across the seas, o'er golden sand.
With hearts ablaze, we'll seize the dawn,
In wandering souls, we are reborn.

## Echoes Beneath the Stars

Beneath the stars, where shadows play,
We find the whispers of yesterday.
Each twinkling light, a tale unfolds,
Of ancient times and secrets told.

In quiet nights, the echoes call,
A gentle breeze, a silken thrall.
We listen close, with hearts attuned,
As cosmic songs in silence croon.

Through starlit paths, our spirits weave,
In every sigh, we dare believe.
The universe speaks in mellow tones,
As heartbeats echo, familiar groans.

With every glance at the midnight sky,
We touch the dreams that never die.
In the tapestry of night so deep,
We gather the promises we keep.

So walk with me beneath these stars,
With open hearts and no more scars.
For in the echoes, we find our way,
Together, let us seize the day.

## Beyond the Boundaries of Light

Stars whisper secrets in the night,
Dreams take flight beyond the sight.
Galaxies spin in cosmic dance,
While shadows drift, lost in trance.

Journeys weave through the ethereal glow,
Time stands still where winds do blow.
Each spark ignites the vast unknown,
Embracing what has yet to be shown.

Across horizons, hearts will soar,
Yearning for what lies evermore.
In the embrace of the infinite skies,
Our spirit's echo forever flies.

When dawn breaks with hues of gold,
The universe reveals tales untold.
Each moment a brushstroke divine,
In the masterpiece of the divine.

So step beyond what eyes can see,
Into the realm of possibility.
For in the darkness, hope ignites,
Beyond the boundaries of light.

## Reflections in the Morning Mist

Softly the dawn paints the sky,
As whispers of mist gently lie.
Nature awakens with grace anew,
In the silence, we find the true.

Mirrored waters hold secrets deep,
Where dreams and reality intertwine and leap.
Each droplet glistens with stories past,
In the heart of the morning, shadows cast.

Birds serenade with melodious tunes,
Embracing the warmth of sunlit dunes.
Crisp air carries a promise sweet,
In every heartbeat, life’s pulse beats.

Footsteps trace paths on dew-kissed grass,
As time flows gently, moments amass.
In the glow, our spirits uplift,
Reflections whisper of life’s gentle gift.

So linger a while in the morning haze,
And cherish the light of the waking days.
Let your heart dance in nature's embrace,
In the stillness, find your place.

**The Canvas of Existence**

Life is a canvas, broad and wide,
Each stroke a journey, a heartfelt ride.
Colors blend with tales untold,
In the tapestry of the brave and bold.

Moments create a vibrant hue,
Every heartbeat resonates true.
The brush of time paints high and low,
Under the sun's warm, golden glow.

Brushstrokes dance in chaotic grace,
Time etches lines upon the face.
With every joy, with every strife,
The canvas holds the essence of life.

From shadows deep to light’s embrace,
Each layer reveals a sacred space.
Under the surface, stories reside,
In the art of living, we confide.

So take the palette of your years,
Mix the colors, laugh the tears.
For in the end, it’s love we paint,
On the canvas of existence, vibrant and quaint.

## Illumination of Untold Stories

In the quiet hush of the night,
Stories flicker, waiting for light.
Echoes of dreams, both near and far,
Whispered softly like a shooting star.

Every heart holds a tale within,
A journey forged through loss and win.
Through tears and laughter, shadows play,
Illuminating the path of the way.

In the silence, voices arise,
Unraveling truths beneath the skies.
Each moment a spark, each memory a flame,
Lighting the paths that bear our name.

As the dawn breaks, stories ignite,
Turning darkness into pure flight.
With every breath, we come alive,
In the illumination, we strive to thrive.

So share your tales, let them flow,
In the garden of life, let the stories grow.
For in the heart of every soul,
Lies the light that makes us whole.

## A Journey through the Veil of Night

Into the depths where shadows creep,
Whispers of silence, secrets to keep.
Starlight glimmers on paths unknown,
Guiding the wanderer, so far from home.

Through tangled woods and misty streams,
Every step echoes forgotten dreams.
The moon casts a spell, soft and bright,
Revealing the magic concealed by night.

Embers of fireflies dance in the dark,
Breathing life into each glowing spark.
A journey unfolds, rich and profound,
In the shadows, adventure is found.

Nature's embrace, both soothing and wild,
The heart of the universe, gentle and mild.
With every breath, we weave and we sway,
In night's tender arms, we drift away.

So take this path, let your fears take flight,
For every journey leads to the light.
Through the veil of night, we stand in awe,
Touched by the beauty that stirs in our core.

## Threads of Sunlight and Moonbeams

Sunrise spills gold on the waking earth,
Glimmers of promise, a new day's birth.
Whispers of morning, soft and sincere,
Draw us from slumber, the time is near.

Threads of sunlight weave through the trees,
Gentle caresses carried by the breeze.
Each leaf dances, kissed by the glow,
In a tapestry formed from nature's flow.

As dusk falls gently, shadows return,
Moonbeams awaken, a mystical burn.
Stars peek through in a sparkling dress,
Inviting our hearts to dream and to guess.

In twilight's embrace, the world holds its breath,
A cycle of light, and a promise of depth.
From sunlight to moon's gentle tease,
Nature hums softly, a sweet, calming breeze.

These threads intertwine, a magical thread,
Bridging the gap where day's light has fled.
In every moment, the universe sings,
Threads of sunlight and moonbeams have wings.

## The Dance of Light and Shadow

In the dawn's embrace, shadows retreat,
Light steps forward, a rhythmic beat.
The sun spins stories on the canvas wide,
Painting the world with colors, a guide.

As day advances, shadows entwine,
In silent whispers, they fall and align.
Together they waltz, in playful disguise,
Under the canopy of boundless skies.

With every movement, a tale unfolds,
In flickering light, and secrets retold.
Shapes blend and blur, in exquisite ballet,
A dance everlasting, where shadows sway.

At dusk, they embrace in a soft, tender kiss,
Light fades away, in a moment of bliss.
Nightfall arrives, with mysteries profound,
The dance of opposites, where wonders abound.

Together they spin, in the cloak of the night,
A world woven tight, in majestic flight.
In light and in shadow, the balance we find,
In the dance of existence, so beautifully twined.

## A Light in Every Window

In every window, a warm, glowing light,
A beacon of hope in the silence of night.
It flickers and dances, inviting the lost,
Reminding us all of the warmth, at what cost.

Stories unfold in each gentle beam,
Whispers of laughter, of love and of dream.
Through crack and through frame, memories cling,
A light in the darkness, a promise of spring.

From candle to lantern, from stitch to thread,
Each light tells a tale, of the words left unsaid.
In times of despair, they gather and glow,
Uniting our hearts in a river of flow.

As the night deepens and shadows encroach,
Each window becomes a comforting coach.
A sanctuary found in the flicker of flame,
Where silence is echoing, yet never the same.

So look to the windows, the lights shining bright,
For within each one, lies a piece of the night.
In every heart's window, love's warmth shall reside,
A light in the darkness, forever our guide.

## The Unseen Canvas of Life

Brushstrokes of dreams paint the sky,
Colors that whisper, time passes by.
Each moment a story, a stroke of fate,
The unseen canvas, where hopes await.

Shadows and light dance on the ground,
In silence, the beauty of life is found.
A palette of choices, vast and wide,
We paint our journeys, with love as our guide.

In laughter and sorrow, in joy and in strife,
Every hue tells the tale of our life.
With each passing day, we create anew,
An artistry woven from dreams that come true.

Through storms and through calm, the colors may fade,
Yet in the heart's canvas, the love will not trade.
Embracing the mess, the beauty and pain,
The unseen canvas knows how to remain.

So pick up your brush, let your spirit soar,
In the gallery of life, there’s always room for more.
With courage and kindness, let your heart blaze,
For in this grand art, we live all our days.

## Voyage into the Expanse

The ship sets sail on unfathomed seas,
With dreams as the compass, and hope as the breeze.
Each wave a whisper, calling us near,
To the depths of the ocean, void of all fear.

Stars twinkle brightly, marking our way,
Guiding the wanderers night and day.
Horizons unfurl like an endless scroll,
As we journey forth, heart, mind, and soul.

The winds of the cosmos, a sweet serenade,
Pulling us deeper into the cascade.
With every crest, we rise and we fall,
To the rhythm of tides, we hear nature's call.

Through tempests and trials, together we stand,
Navigating wonders, hand in hand.
For the voyage is precious, a tale yet untold,
In the expanse of the universe, courage unfolds.

So raise your sails high, let the adventure begin,
In the voyage of life, let the magic seep in.
With eyes full of wonder, and hearts open wide,
We'll explore this expanse, our dreams as our guide.

## Stars That Guide the Heart

In the quiet of night, the stars align,
Whispers of the universe, a sacred sign.
They sparkle with secrets, deep in their glow,
Illuminating paths that we yearn to know.

Each star a wish, a promise held tight,
Guiding us gently through shadows of night.
With every shimmer, a heartbeat we find,
A connection to dreams intertwined.

This celestial dance, a tapestry spun,
Threads of our stories, together as one.
In moments of doubt, we lift up our gaze,
And find in their brilliance, courage to blaze.

The cosmos a map, where our spirits roam,
The stars that we seek, they lead us back home.
So trust in their light, as you journey afar,
For love is the compass, and dreams are the stars.

Let their luminescence guide you each night,
Through valleys of sorrow, to peaks of pure light.
In the tapestry woven, we're never apart,
For it's the stars that guide the heart.

## The Call of the Unknown

Amidst the stillness, a whisper comes clear,
The call of the unknown, drawing us near.
It beckons our spirits, ignites the spark,
To venture beyond, into the dark.

Each step into mystery, we rise with the tide,
Embracing the thrill of the wild, untied.
For in every shadow, there shines a light,
A truth waiting quietly, within the night.

The journey unfolds, a map yet unseen,
In the depths of our hearts, we're brave and serene.
With questions like stars, we seek and explore,
For in every answer, there's always more.

With courage as armor, we face what is real,
The call of the unknown is a powerful wheel.
As we wander through realms of wonder and awe,
We find in the journey, our spirit's true law.

So heed the soft call, let your heart lead the way,
For the unknown awaits, in the light of the day.
With dreams as your compass, embrace the vast sea,
In the call of the unknown, we are truly free.

## The Palette of Possibilities

Colors blend upon the screen,
Dreams of what might yet be seen.
Each brushstroke carries hope anew,
A canvas vast, inviting you.

Whispers of adventure call,
In hues that rise and softly fall.
Every shade a tale to share,
To paint a future bright and fair.

In shadows deep, in light so bright,
We find our path and seek the light.
A mosaic crafted from our heart,
In this grand journey, we partake.

Brush in hand, we take the chance,
To let our dreams begin to dance.
With every stroke, new worlds ignite,
Our spirit soars, embraced by night.

Life's a canvas, vast and wide,
With every moment, we decide.
What colors speak, what tales we tell,
In the palette, we dwell so well.

**Seeking the Sun's Embrace**

Golden rays break through the dawn,
A gentle touch on grassy lawn.
Warmth awakens every soul,
In the sunlight, we are whole.

Chasing shadows, we pursue,
Moments wrapped in gleaming hue.
Each heartbeat echoes, soft and clear,
A melody for all to hear.

Embrace the light, let worries part,
Feel the sun’s warmth in your heart.
Fleeting clouds may drift away,
But in sunlight, we shall stay.

Together, we dance through the day,
As golden beams light up our way.
In every shimmer, dreams take flight,
In every heartbeat, pure delight.

Hold this warmth, let love ignite,
In the sun's embrace, we find our sight.
Journey forward, hand in hand,
As we wander through this land.

## Wings of the Inner Voyager

Within the depths, a journey starts,
A flight of mind, a dance of hearts.
With wings unseen, we rise and soar,
Into the realms of evermore.

Exploring thoughts, uncharted lands,
Where imagination's magic stands.
Through valleys deep and mountains high,
Our spirits glimmer, touch the sky.

The whispers of the cosmos call,
In every rise, we learn to fall.
In stillness found, our answers dwell,
In every story, we can tell.

With courage bold, we break the chains,
And find the strength that still remains.
Wings unfurling, boldly we glide,
In the vastness, we will take pride.

The inner voyager knows no bounds,
In silence deep, a truth resounds.
Through every journey, wisdom grows,
In the heart's embrace, the spirit flows.

## Where the Sky Meets the Soul

At the horizon, dreams collide,
Where earth meets heaven's graceful ride.
In every sunset, hope renews,
Painting the sky in vibrant hues.

Clouds drift softly, whispers flow,
Secrets of the winds we know.
In every glance, we feel the pull,
Of skyward thoughts that make us whole.

Beneath the stars, our wishes rise,
Reflections bright in midnight skies.
In twilight's glow, we find our peace,
A calm within that will not cease.

From dawn to dusk, the cycle turns,
In every heart, a passion burns.
Where earth and sky in silence meet,
The essence lies, profound and sweet.

In this vast space, we find our place,
Each moment rich, a soft embrace.
Where the sky meets soul, we belong,
In harmony, we weave our song.

## Veins of the Universe

Stars pulse above in night’s embrace,
Galaxies swirl, a vast, dark space.
Light-years drift like whispers slow,
In the cosmic dance, we ebb and flow.

Nebulas bloom in colors bright,
Painting the void with dreams of light.
Wormholes beckon with secret signs,
In the heart of space, the truth aligns.

Time unwinds, a thread so fine,
Each moment crafted, a grand design.
Like rivers of stardust, we intertwine,
In the veins of the universe, we brightly shine.

Echoes of creation softly sing,
From darkness birthed, the cosmos spring.
In everything, a part of we,
Boundless, infinite, eternity.

Eyes turned skyward, seeking grace,
In the heavens, we find our place.
Rich with wonder, the night unveils,
The mysteries held in stellar trails.

## Shadows Dancing at Dusk

Flickering light as day starts to wane,
Whispers of night in the cooling rain.
Shadows elongate, merge, and sway,
In the twilight's embrace, they play.

Trees bend low, the wind’s gentle caress,
Each branch a story, each leaf a guess.
Casting silhouettes as dreams take flight,
Silent whispers fill the encroaching night.

Stars awaken, one by one,
Bidding farewell to the setting sun.
In the dusky veil, secrets unfurl,
Shadows dancing in a midnight whirl.

Night's cool breath wraps the world so tight,
As the moon spills silver, the dark ignites.
Stories woven in whispers soft,
In shadows dancing, our spirits aloft.

Each moment fleeting, yet time suspends,
In the dusk’s glow, all sorrow mends.
Life's fleeting dance, a mystical trust,
In shadows dancing, we find what’s just.

## Ascending Through the Ether

Winds of change cradle the soul,
Through the ether, we seek our role.
Ascend we must, beyond the pain,
In the heights, there's much to gain.

Clouds part gently, revealing light,
Guiding us ever beyond the night.
Infinite whispers, a call divine,
In the ethereal vastness, we intertwine.

Echoes of laughter from worlds unknown,
In the currents of air, our dreams are sown.
With each soft breath, we rise and glide,
In the ether’s arms, we will abide.

Fleeting moments turn to echoes sweet,
Loss and longing, we bravely meet.
Each ascent a tapestry woven fine,
In the ether’s dance, our hearts align.

Sailing on hopes we paint the skies,
Through the ether, we learn to rise.
In every star, a beacon’s glow,
Ascending through dreams, we come to know.

## Dreams in the Twilight

In the twilight, whispers softly gleam,
Carried on winds of a fading dream.
Colors blend as day meets night,
In the hush, we find true insight.

Stars awaken, patience in their glow,
In twilight's arms, new visions grow.
Scripting tales in shadowed grace,
Every heart beats in this sacred space.

Glancing back at the day’s embrace,
Hopes stretch out, in time and place.
Dreams ignite like fireflies' dance,
Twilight whispers of fate and chance.

With each breath, the night unfurls,
In soft murmurs, the magic swirls.
In the twilight, all paths align,
A canvas painted, so pure, divine.

In dreams we find the courage to soar,
In the twilight’s tender lore.
Embracing the night, our spirits take flight,
In the dance of dreams, we find our light.

**A Tapestry of Dreams and Yearnings**

In the quiet of the night, we weave,
Threads of hope and love, we believe.
Colors bright in softest hues,
Each dream a path, we choose to cruise.

Together we stitch our tales so bright,
Embroidered whispers in the pale moonlight.
Through gentle hands, our stories flow,
A tapestry rich, where wishes grow.

With every stitch a secret shared,
In the fabric of time, we dared.
Patterns formed by heart's embrace,
As longing finds its cherished place.

In twilight's glow, our visions dance,
Fleeting moments, a fleeting chance.
We gather pieces, bits of gold,
In the warmth of dreams, we unfold.

United by threads unseen,
In the canvas of life, we glean.
Each yearning sewn, a gentle thread,
A tapestry bright, where dreams are fed.

## Footprints on the Waves of Time

Upon the shore, we leave our marks,
Footprints fading, like fleeting sparks.
The ocean whispers tales of old,
In tides of silver, stories told.

Each wave a chapter, ebb and flow,
Moments captured, lost, and slow.
The sea, a mirror to our dreams,
Reflects our hopes, our silent screams.

As sands of time slip through our hands,
We trace our past on distant lands.
With every tide, a choice we make,
In the dance of life, we bend, we break.

The horizon beckons, wide and deep,
A canvas vast for us to keep.
Ghostly echoes of laughter ring,
In every wave, the memories cling.

So let us walk where sea meets sky,
In every moment, let us fly.
For footprints fade but hearts will stay,
In the ocean's embrace, come what may.

## The Call of the Unseen

In shadows deep, the silence calls,
Echoes linger as nightfall falls.
A whisper dances in the air,
The unseen beckons, soft and rare.

Through tangled paths, my spirit roams,
Chasing sighs of dreams and homes.
With every heartbeat, secrets pulse,
A longing deep, a timeless impulse.

The veil between worlds, thin and frail,
In twilight's glow, we weave the tale.
Mysteries stir in velvet night,
Guided by stars, we seek the light.

The call of the unseen echoes loud,
In the space where dreams are proud.
Awakening senses, wild and free,
Within the depths of what could be.

We follow the threads, the cosmic seam,
In the silence, we find our dream.
Entwined in wonder, we shall find,
The call of the unseen, ever kind.

## Between the Stars and the Sea

Under the blanket of night’s embrace,
We wander far, in time and space.
Between the stars, the ocean's breath,
Lies a world of dreams, beyond death.

The sea reflects the skies above,
A mirror of hope, a symbol of love.
In every wave, a wish set free,
Drifting gently, like thoughts on the sea.

Constellations call from high above,
Guiding our hearts, like a dove.
We sail through shadows, pierce the gloom,
In the cosmic dance, we find our bloom.

Whispers of dreams ride on the tide,
Ebb and flow, like life’s wild ride.
We gather stardust, blend and mix,
Between two worlds, the secrets fix.

So let us wander, hand in hand,
Through star-kissed skies and ocean's sand.
For in this space, our spirits rise,
Between the stars and sea, we fly.

## Whispers of the Infinite Sky

In twilight's embrace, stars softly sigh,
Moonlight drapes clouds as they drift by.
Infinite stories in dark they unfurl,
Whispers of dreams in the vastness swirl.

Night's silent canvas, painted with light,
Constellations dance in the still of the night.
Each spark a secret, a wish, a plea,
In the ocean of ether, forever free.

A lullaby murmurs through cool, gentle air,
As lovers of midnight breathe in the rare.
With every heartbeat, they feel the pull,
Of galaxies spinning, beautiful, full.

Echoes of silence ring deep in the heart,
Awakening spirits that never depart.
In the arms of the cosmos, tender and wide,
The whispers of starlight remain as our guide.

So let us lay back and gaze at the show,
In the cradle of night, where dreams gently flow.
For within this expanse, where the wild wonders fly,
We are but whispers, beneath the infinite sky.

## Silent Seas of Stardust

In depths of the night, where silence abides,
Sailing through stardust, on cosmic tides.
Waves of the cosmos, they shimmer and gleam,
Navigating softly, lost in a dream.

The nebula's glow, a lantern in the dark,
Guiding the vessels with soft, gentle spark.
In stillness we drift, uncharted and free,
In silent seas woven from shadows and light.

Each star is a beacon, each planet a guide,
In this tranquil haven, let our spirits glide.
Together we wander through voids vast and wide,
Connected by starlight, forever side by side.

As comets sweep past, tales whisper in breeze,
Of worlds that are waiting, of souls and of trees.
In the heart of the universe, stories reside,
In silent seas of stardust, where dreams coincide.

So let us embark on this journey sublime,
With hope as our compass, transcending all time.
For in the embrace of the infinite night,
We find love and wonder, our spirits take flight.

## Echoes of Tomorrow's Dawn

When night meets the day, whispers can be heard,
Soft echoes of futures, in silence conferred.
Hopes are born anew, as dreams take their flight,
In the fragile moments that blend dark and light.

Each sunrise a canvas, fresh stories to paint,
With strokes of ambition, and colors of grace.
The shadows recede, making way for the sun,
As echoes of tomorrow's dawn have begun.

In the gentle whispers, we find our own truth,
Guided by visions, the fire of youth.
In every heartbeat, a promise resides,
Of possibilities waiting, like oceanic tides.

The morning unfurls with a delicate glow,
Inviting the dreams that in stillness we sow.
With faith as our lantern, we reach for the skies,
In echoes of morning, our spirits will rise.

For tomorrow is painted in hues of our choice,
In the symphony of life, we listen, rejoice.
As the sun breaks the horizon, its warmth gently drawn,
We gather the echoes of tomorrow's dawn.

### Boundless Dreams in Still Waters

In tranquil reflections, dreams swim like fish,
Rippling through silence, fulfilling each wish.
The still waters cradle, as thoughts start to flow,
Boundless and free, where the soft whispers go.

Underneath the surface, secrets unfold,
Stories of ages, both timid and bold.
In this liquid realm, where the heart knows to seek,
Live the visions that quietly speak.

Each droplet a fragment, a piece of the whole,
Mirroring dreams that awaken the soul.
With every soft wave, a heartbeat aligned,
In boundless dreams where the stars are defined.

The moon hangs above, a guardian bright,
Illuminating pathways to future's delight.
In stillness we ponder, our hopes intertwined,
In the fabric of night, where our hearts are enshrined.

So close your eyes softly, let visions reside,
In boundless dreams where the spirit can glide.
For still waters whisper of worlds yet unseen,
In the dance of the cosmic, forever serene.

**Tales From the Whispering Winds**

In the hush of night, a secret sigh,
Leaves dance softly, under the sky.
Each gust carries stories, long and old,
Whispers of dreams, that never get told.

Beneath the moonlight, shadows play,
Echoes of laughter, drifting away.
They weave through the trees, a gentle hum,
Nature’s own music, to which we succumb.

The winds stretch wide, across the land,
Sharing the tales, so bravely planned.
Voices of ages, in breathless flight,
Calling us home, to the heart of night.

Carried on breezes, the legends flow,
Each a reminder, of times we know.
Tales of the brave, and those who dreamt,
In the heart of the winds, their spirits leapt.

So listen closely, in the quiet hours,
To the stories hidden, amongst the flowers.
For the winds may share, if we dare to pause,
The rich tapestry, of life’s wondrous cause.

## The Awakening of Forgotten Stars

In the velvet night, they softly gleam,
Dreams of the cosmos, on a silvery beam.
Forgotten whispers, from ages past,
Awakening softly, their light holds fast.

Through the dark voids, where silence reigned,
Each star a promise, patiently gained.
Their twinkling eyes, hold secrets untold,
Of worlds unknown, and fables bold.

With every blink, they dance in time,
Rhythms of ages, in perfect rhyme.
Once overlooked, they boldly shine,
Revealing the magic, of the divine.

Feel the pulse of the night, as they rise,
Painting the heavens, with bright surprise.
Stars awaken, casting their spells,
In the stillness of night, their voices swell.

So gaze upon skies, where wonders dwell,
Listen to stories, they long to tell.
For in the darkness, they light our way,
The forgotten stars, will never fray.

## In Search of the Hidden Dawn

Through shadows deep, we wander still,
Chasing the light, with steadfast will.
Each step we take, leads closer, near,
To the hidden dawn, we hold so dear.

Misty horizons, softly glow,
Hints of promise, in the night's shadow.
A rustle of leaves, whispers so slight,
Guiding our hearts, back to the light.

As night recedes, a soft embrace,
The horizon blushes, a warming grace.
Golden rays, break through the veil,
In search of dawn, we cannot fail.

With hope as our compass, and dreams as our guide,
We'll journey forth, with love as our tide.
To find the dawn, where life begins,
In the quiet moment, our story spins.

So follow the whispers, let them unfold,
The tale of dawn, waiting to be told.
For in each sunrise, a new chance gleams,
In search of the hidden dawn, we chase our dreams.

## The Pulse of Cosmic Currents

In the depths of space, a rhythm flows,
Cosmic currents, with mysteries close.
A symphony rising, beyond the sight,
Echos of creation, in the still of night.

Stars collide and shimmer, in dance divine,
Each pulse a heartbeat, in the fabric of time.
Galaxies twirl, in a waltz so grand,
Writing their stories, with an unseen hand.

Feel the energy, that moves through us all,
In the silence of starlight, we heed the call.
For we are made, of this very dust,
Connected through time, in this we trust.

Ride the waves of this cosmic song,
Where every note belongs, where we are strong.
In the depths of the cosmos, a pulse resides,
A dance of creation, where love abides.

So flow with the currents, let your spirit soar,
Join the vast chorus, forever explore.
For the pulse of the universe beats within,
In the realms of the cosmic, we all begin.

**The Veil Between Worlds**

In whispers soft, the shadows creep,
A threshold drawn where secrets sleep.
A flicker of light, a distant call,
Beyond the rim of the known and all.

With steps unsure, we venture near,
To grasp the wild, to face the fear.
The veil hangs thick, a gossamer thread,
Linking the living and those who’ve fled.

Echoes of laughter, a haunting sigh,
The stories linger, they never die.
In twilight’s grasp, the worlds entwine,
A dance of shadows, a spark divine.

With open hearts, we pierce the gloom,
In quests of souls, new blooms will bloom.
The veil may shimmer, it may obscure,
Yet love transcends, a light so pure.

So take my hand, let’s cross this line,
Embrace the unknown where fates align.
Through the veil, we shall chime,
In between worlds, we’ll write our rhyme.

## Resonance of the Celestial Heart

In the hush of night, stars hum a tune,
A symphony sung beneath the moon.
With cosmic threads, our hearts align,
In the vastness, an embrace divine.

Each heartbeat echoes through the void,
A pulse of beauty, none destroyed.
As galaxies swirl in waltz so bright,
We dance in shadows, bathed in light.

Nebulas whisper their age-old lore,
Wisdom and wonder forever explore.
With colors vibrant, the heavens spread,
In every heartbeat, the voices tread.

A cosmic bond, unbreakable chains,
Galactic love that flows in veins.
In the resonance, we find our part,
Together we breathe, the celestial heart.

So gaze above, let your spirit soar,
In the stellar glow, we are ever more.
In the cosmos' grip, we find our place,
Hearts intertwined in endless space.

## Colors of a Dreamer's Sky

A tapestry sprawls, the dreamer's flight,
With hues of hope, in gentle light.
Pastel whispers paint the dawn,
While starlit echoes linger on.

With strokes of gold, the sun ascends,
A promise held, where daylight bends.
Each color swirls, a vibrant sigh,
In the heart of a dreamer's sky.

Indigo nights weave tales so grand,
Of worlds unseen, of souls that stand.
In fields of azure, where wishes play,
A brush of magic fills the gray.

With every hue, a story spun,
In a dreamer's heart, the journey's begun.
Through crimson clouds and twilight blue,
The palette whispers of wishes true.

So lift your gaze, let dreams take flight,
In the canvas made by the soft night light.
For in the colors, the heart will pry,
The endless tales of a dreamer's sky.

## Light Beyond the Distant Verge

At the edge of dusk, where shadows blend,
A flickering beacon, a call to mend.
Beyond the verge, where dreams ignite,
A promise glowing, against the night.

With every step into the unknown,
The heart's bright flame will be our own.
In whispers low, the stars reflect,
The path unfolding, what we select.

With courage found, we face the fear,
For light will guide us, always near.
In the vast expanse, we seek the truth,
In every heartbeat, the dance of youth.

And when the dawn breaks soft and clear,
We'll cherish the journey, hold it dear.
For light beyond, forever will call,
From distant verges, we'll answer all.

So heed the call of the radiant day,
Chase the shadows gently away.
With every dawn, our spirits surge,
In the light beyond the distant verge.

www.ingramcontent.com/pod-product-compliance
Ingram Content Group UK Ltd.
Pitfield, Milton Keynes, MK11 3LW, UK
UKHW032216171224
452513UK00010B/484

9 789908 126128